Create your own
elegant Interior!
-XOXO-
Sallie Kjos p.53

CREATING ELEGANT INTERIORS

Designers in their Own Words

MELISSA MATHER

CREATING ELEGANT INTERIORS

Designers in their Own Words

MELISSA MATHER

GRAY and BOARDMAN
PRESS

Contents

FOREWORD

The ability to express your personal style through the design of the interior of your home is powerful. And when it is accomplished, everyone who passes through your doors will take notice — no matter the size or value of your home.

Stylish interior design is not about wealth or expensive furnishings and accessories. During my twenty-five years in the design industry, I've seen large homes that feel drab and generic and small cottages that feel polished and refined.

Creating an elegant interior for your home, whether you do it alone or with the assistance of an interior designer, is rooted in knowing yourself and surrounding yourself with the things that make you feel beautiful and comforted.

But most importantly, it is about having the courage to create and project that beauty and comfort inside your home.

Diane Tomaczak

ACKNOWLEDGEMENTS

With deepest gratitude we thank
Martha Bullen, Cari Shane, Sherry Moeller,
Marilyn Campbell and Rhonda Fleming.

INTRODUCTION

Imagine walking into a room that is breathtakingly lovely. The vision of what that room looks like is different for each one of us. That's what makes interior design style so elusive. It's easy to recognize, but it's hard to describe. And it's even harder to create.

In this book, talented designers offer some of the insights they use while guiding their clients to the discovery of their own unique design style. These designers strive to create interiors that reflect not only their clients' style, but also the way in which they live their lives and who they are as individuals.

Creating Elegant Interiors presents questions to a variety of skillful tastemakers, each with a discerning eye for style. Their answers are intended to help you begin your journey to discovering your own sense of style and creating a home that is not only aesthetically appealing, but also comfortable and livable.

This book offers a collection of narratives from interior design experts — their individual answers to the same set of questions. Our intention is to offer advice in each designer's own words and to share with you trade secrets for creating an interior that reflects your own personal style.

VICTORIA SANCHEZ

First and foremost, I can never sacrifice beauty,
and neither should you!

Identifying your Personal Style

I always tell my clients, "Let's start with one of your favorite things in the house for inspiration." It can be art, a bowl, a pillow, or even a special something inherited through the family. Your favorite things are a direct reflection of your personal style. When you start there, everything else just falls into place.

Questions to Ask When Starting a Design Project

I always ask lifestyle questions early on in the design process to understand how my clients want to best use their space. For example, do you have a big family that requires ten seats at the dining table? Do you host the weekly playgroup and therefore need open spaces and childproof fabrics?

Write down your answers and you will quickly see what you need and what's important to you, and this will help you develop the right space.

Guidelines for Creating an Elegant but Comfortable Space

I never sacrifice beauty, and neither should you. Elegant style can always live side by side with function. There are many wonderful stain-resistant fabrics available, and investing in one can give you peace of mind without compromising quality and style. Also, stay away from finishes and surfaces that show every scratch and ding. Gently distressed surfaces help hide everyday life.

Style Elements that Create a Timeless and Classic Home Decor

My secret for timeless interiors is actually quite simple: My bigger investment pieces always honor classic elements that we have seen for centuries in every form of design. That's why I call my style modern traditional.

Your grandmother's dining room sideboard can be given updated glamour with a black lacquer paint job, new hardware, and glass lamps. Trendy pieces are always fun and tempting and perfect to use in small doses, such as pillows, a bedside lamp, or an occasional table.

Identifying your Personal Style

Pull out inspiration photos from magazines and circle or note the elements of the design that you like. It's often difficult to determine our personal styles, but once you point out specific things you like, you can start to build a pattern that helps identify your style. That could be comfortable casual, classic and formal, easy and natural, or crisp and modern.

Questions to Ask When Starting a Design Project

One of the first things to ask and consider is how the space is going to be used. Will it be adults only in a formal setting or a space with children and pets?

From there, I recommend identifying spaces or things in your current home that you enjoy. Recognize what it is about those things that makes you happy, whether it's a comfortable sofa the whole family can sit on together, a certain color or texture that you love, or a piece of art that reflects a certain mood.

It's important to give your home personality and add elements that you enjoy.

Guidelines for Creating an Elegant but Comfortable Space

A livable space often means incorporating fabrics and textures that wear well. That could include washable cotton slipcovers, which can be very elegant when made well, or possibly Sunbrella indoor fabrics, which can be very stylish and are totally stain resistant.

Plan seating to accommodate the amount of people who will use the space on a daily basis, and then incorporate additional seating for entertaining, such as cube ottomans or exposed wood side chairs.

It's so important to measure before purchasing. In fact, there are multiple software programs that allow you to insert your room dimensions and then input your furniture pieces to ensure that everything fits properly.

Style Elements that Create a Timeless and Classic Home Decor

Choosing neutrals for sofas and stained woods or neutral paints for case goods like tables and chests can extend the longevity of those pieces and help maintain a timeless, classic look.

Don't ignore pattern, but put trendier patterns or more current colors on smaller pieces that can easily be recovered, such as dining chairs or armchairs, or on accessories that can be changed down the road, like lamps, throw pillows, and affordable floor coverings.

Final Thoughts

It's important to give your home personality and add elements that you enjoy. If you don't love something, you shouldn't put it in your home unless it truly serves a purpose.

It's also important not to decorate your home too quickly. Live in your space, get a feel for how rooms function in your life, and then start to decide how best to decorate and furnish.

It's okay to slowly collect pieces over time to create your own personal look. This also allows you to invest in quality pieces that you can use for many years.

DAVID ANTHONY CHENAULT

Identifying your Personal Style

I look for prints, color combinations, and the details that my clients love in their wardrobes, and translate a few of those elements into the design details.

Questions to Ask When Starting a Design Project

When I consult with new clients, I ask a series of questions, including, "What do you have in your closet or hanging in your home right now that you see yourself still wearing or still owning in 5 to 10 years? What is it about that piece or style that draws you to it? Is it the patterns, lines, textures or some other element?"

Guidelines for Creating an Elegant but Comfortable Space

Usually my clients have already discovered who they are and what they want to be around on a daily basis. I truly feel that people are an extension of their homes and that most know what they look good in and feel good in.

If I get a young client who has not been exposed to style much, I usually pull from what they like now, and then go back to what they have been drawn to since their interest in style and fashion began. They may experiment, but they usually come back to where they started, often with something new to add to it. This experience brings their own personal twist to their look. It's fun for clients to finish a project and to learn a few things about themselves along the way.

Style Elements that Create a Timeless and Classic Home Decor

When I'm designing a home, I'm always striving for something that is timelessly classic. I don't think you can design for the present without looking back at the past and thinking about the future. I do not do a trendy style.

*I look for prints, color combinations, and the details
that my clients love in their wardrobes....*

JOHN BROWN

Identifying your Personal Style

To identify your personal style, look at design magazines and books and see what resonates with you. Personally, I am always inspired by fine hotels and how their interiors make me feel.

Questions to Ask When Starting a Design Project

Are you attracted to very specific styles or do you prefer a more collected look? Do you want to incorporate pieces that you have discovered on your travels?

What colors appeal to you? This is so important. Different colors can make your mood. Consider your color needs for different rooms: relaxing for the bedroom, possibly bolder in the dining room.

Personal needs are different for different clients. How do you want to use your rooms? How many people do you want to seat in your living room and dining room? How do you entertain?

You can't have elegance without comfort or your home becomes a museum.

Guidelines for Creating an Elegant but Comfortable Space

You can't have elegance without comfort or your home becomes a museum. Invest in good quality sofas and chairs. Well-made furnishings can last a lifetime. Just reupholster in the future.

Style Elements that Create a Timeless and Classic Home Decor

Timeless interiors include some of my favorite items: mahogany, leather, bone, and blue and white porcelain – I love the elegance of a crisp Chinese blue. Orchids are always fabulous and flowers wake up a room. Rooms need to smell wonderful, and if you are not using fresh flowers, I love to scent a room with candles and/or diffusers.

Some of my favorite fabrics come from Scalamandre, Anichini, and Fortuny. I like historical references in my designs: Antique-framed Italian intaglios, 17th- and 18th- century framed prints, and Persian carpets always have a timeless appeal.

KERRIE KELLY

By being eclectic, we resist being limited…

Identifying your Personal Style

What kind of place do you want to come home to? It should be a space that is comfortable, welcoming, and a reflection of your style and taste, a space that's uniquely yours. The key to such a space is great design.

There isn't just one way to design a room, nor is there one style that is best for a particular space, however. Good design is personal. Good rooms are livable, and should convey the sense that the person who designed them made thoughtful aesthetic decisions and then embraced those decisions.

Great rooms evolve as we live in them, reflecting the stories of our lives. But before you can design such rooms, you need to gain a basic knowledge of the main principles of design and the elements present in different design styles, and understand how to pull those elements together. Rooms should be both functional and beautiful, as well as exciting to look at, pleasing to be in, and welcoming to family and friends.

These concepts apply whether you're decorating an entire house or refreshing a room with new paint or upholstery.

Questions to Ask When Starting a Design Project

An interesting thing happens when you ask people, even designers, to describe their decorating styles. Often they freeze and then blurt out, "Um, I don't know – eclectic?" Eclectic has come to mean, "I have my own personal style. I mix things together, old and new, classic and modern, things that I like." By being eclectic, we resist being limited like we would be if we said, "I'm a traditionalist," or "My style is contemporary."

We may make mistakes, but we keep trying until we settle into rooms that we feel express ourselves. Fortunately, today's best designs, even those with a specific style, reflect this.

Understanding the basic components of three major styles will help you lay the underpinnings for a well-designed room that reflects your personality and taste: traditional, modern, and transitional.

No matter what style you prefer, understanding basic design principles will help you create a space that is both inviting and pleasing...

Guidelines for Creating an Elegant but Comfortable Space

Before you rush out to buy paint and furniture, take some time to evaluate your space and plan your changes. There are no hard and fast rules for where to begin and what to look at, but this room function checklist is a start.

- Is it a well-used and casual room or a more formal space?
- Are pets welcome?
- What time of day is the space used?
- What activities go on in this room?
- Who uses the space?
- What are the views?
- Are there structural, plumbing, or electrical issues?
- What do you like about the existing space? What do you dislike?
- What is your budget?

Style Elements that Create a Timeless and Classic Home Decor

No matter what style you prefer, understanding basic design principles will help you create a space that is both inviting and pleasing, one that catches and holds your attention. These principles include balance, scale and proportion, rhythm, emphasis, and harmony.

Some people naturally understand balance, which is using symmetry to lend a gracious feel to a space and then throwing things off with exactly the right asymmetry, just enough to keep things interesting. Others know instinctively about scale and proportion. Still others seem to be able to create a sense of rhythm or to choose just the right focal points to add emphasis to parts of the space.

When these elements of design work together seamlessly, there is harmony in the room. And a harmonious room is one that is inviting, comfortable, and livable – in other words, the best kind of room to be in.

Final Thoughts

Some people have a clear vision and are confident about decorating, while others find the prospect daunting. Whether you consider the process exciting or intimidating, the steps are the same: dream first, explore your options, and then create a plan that will allow you to reach your goal, with enough flexibility in both plan and budget to allow the unexpected.

KERRA MICHELE HUERTA

Identifying your Personal Style

Start by opening your closet: What colors do you see most? What types of fabrics? What style of shoes?

If your closet is filled with white fur coats and stilettos, you will have a very different type of space than a person who prefers jeans and sneakers. Putting a room together is like getting dressed, just on a larger scale. If you stick with a color palette that reflects what's in your closet, you know you'll always look great in your own home.

Questions to Ask When Starting a Design Project

Ask yourself, "How do I use my space?" Just because a room was intended for a specific purpose doesn't mean that applies to you. For example, if you're a musician with a spare bedroom, and you rarely host overnight guests, the room may work better as a music studio. If you have a formal dining room but prefer to eat out, consider adding a wall of bookcases and a couple of comfy reading chairs to create a luxurious library.

Guidelines for Creating an Elegant but Comfortable Space

I often go into new clients' homes and they're filled with furniture and accessories that they thought they should buy, but didn't love. Don't try too hard. Don't over-think it. Instead, focus on adding items that you love and add meaning to your life.

Style Elements that Create a Timeless and Classic Home Decor

Neutral, monochromatic spaces will be classic forever. If you're working without the help of a professional, and want more color, I always suggest sticking to neutrals for large pieces like sofas and chairs, and using accessories to introduce colors, patterns, and trends.

*Focus on adding items that you love
and add meaning to your life.*

Courtney Thomas

Identifying your Personal Style

Start with a neutral palette and add some personality through accessories. By adding elements that reflect who you are, it's easy to make your space unique and personal.

But by keeping the bones neutral, it's easy to change the look of the room as your tastes change, without having to invest in major pieces.

Of course, if you have a statement piece that you want to include, such as a brightly colored sofa or patterned chairs, use it. The space should really be about things you love.

Questions to Ask When Starting a Design Project

I always follow the rule that if something really speaks to me, I buy it. If it's something you really love, there will always be a spot for it.

Think about what you want to be the focal point of the room. Do you have a meaningful piece that you want to feature? If so, what's the best way to feature it?

Guidelines for Creating an Elegant but Comfortable Space

Know when to splurge and when to save. Invest in quality key pieces that will get daily use, like a sofa or a kitchen table. It's worth a little extra money up front to know that you have a piece that will last for years. You can balance out the extra spending by filling in the space with less expensive accessories. Local boutiques are a great source for unique furniture and accessories.

Style Elements that Create a Timeless and Classic Home Decor

Books are a great accessory for any room and can be used in many ways beyond the traditional bookshelf. Stand a row of books on a desk or console table and add interesting bookends. Stack a few larger books on an end table to add height to a lamp. Even just a couple of books on the coffee table add interest.

A mirror is another timeless accessory. With so many varieties to choose from, they are perfect for any style. Prop a mirror on the mantel instead of a picture. Hang a mirror opposite a window in a small space to help reflect the light and make the room feel bigger. Tuck a small mirror in a bookcase or cabinet.

MOLLY BRUNO

Make decisions based on your lifestyle and your needs
rather than what you think is on trend.

Identifying your Personal Style

Review your family's needs and what is important to you. How a space functions is as important as how it looks. For example, a family room that looks beautiful but shows every mud stain will not work for a family with young children.

As far as cultivating your personal decorating style, look to your closet for inspiration: Your decorating aesthetic will often mirror your tastes in clothing and personal style.

Questions to Ask When Starting a Design Project

Some of the questions you should ask yourself are:

- Does the area get a lot of foot traffic?
- Are you a homebody?
- Is the space used for work as well as relaxing?

Make decisions based on your lifestyle and your needs rather than what you think is on trend.

Guidelines for Creating an Elegant but Comfortable Space

Finish your windows. Whether it's a bamboo shade flanked by a pleated curtain or a simple Roman shade, window treatments offer a sense of completeness.

Pay attention to textiles. For upholstery, use rich fabrics such as velvet and linen, which can withstand a lot of wear and tear while looking fantastic.

Natural fiber rugs are low maintenance and refined, making them a great choice.

Don't forget the accessories: Large throw pillows in a whimsical fabric can tie a space together and add an instant layer of lushness.

Style Elements that Create a Timeless and Classic Home Decor

Get rid of harsh overhead lighting. Replace outdated ceiling fixtures with low, lantern-style pendants or simply use low-wattage light bulbs.

Final Thoughts

Have fun with it. Your home should calm you down, not stress you out.

How much time do you plan to spend in the space?
Do you see this as a private retreat or a public space
where you would welcome company?

Identifying your Personal Style

Personal touches and do-it-yourself projects are great ways to showcase your tastes and sense of style. Don't be afraid to use your space as a creative outlet. Do-it-yourself projects don't need to be super time-consuming or terribly sophisticated, either.

Questions to Ask When Starting a Design Project

How much time do you plan to spend in the space? Do you see this as a private retreat or a public space where you would welcome company? Should this be a space to relax and be free of technology, or do you want to be dialed in and connected at all times?

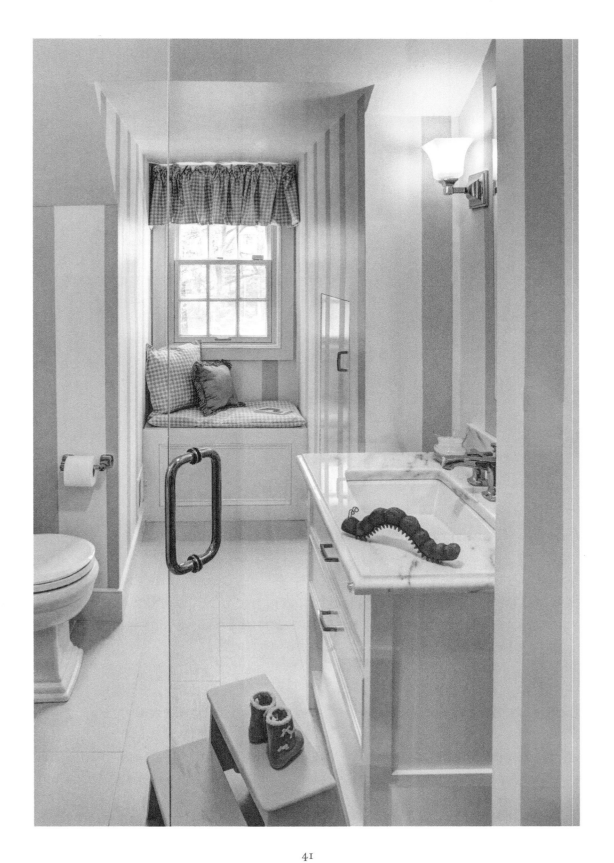

Guidelines for Creating an Elegant but Comfortable Space

Consider what is livable to you. A beautiful sofa will only be beautiful for so long if you don't choose a fabric that will wear well with lots of use, is pet-friendly, and won't fade with exposure to sunlight. Consider paying a little more and investing in quality, well-constructed pieces that you will treasure for years to come.

Style Elements that Create a Timeless and Classic Home Decor

Choose fixtures and finishes that lean toward the transitional side. Many folks install marble in kitchens or bathrooms because the material is generally considered timeless and less likely to date a space or go out of style.

Consider paying a little more and investing in quality,
well-constructed pieces that you will treasure for years to come.

Identifying your Personal Style

Discovering your personal style is often very different than identifying your needs in the home. Clients may want all-white upholstery or to show off their many antique soup tureens. But if they have children or pets, that style will only result in frustration. Truly stylish spaces need to be functional as well as beautiful.

Do the clients want a formal living room or a room perfect for casual pizza and game night? Do they want a dedicated guest bedroom or do they need a home office with a sleep sofa?

Perhaps a smaller space requires multiple uses. If so, the clients will have to prioritize their needs. Then we can discuss wants. That is when your personal style can emerge.

Let your home make you happy.
Walking into your home should be like getting a hug.

Questions to Ask When Starting a Design Project

How the space will be used is number one on the list, followed by budget. Establish an overall budget, but leave room for flexibility between rooms or for a special piece of art or furniture that may catch your eye.

It's also important to establish the type of furniture you need. Do you regularly host lots of family and friends? Maybe a sectional sofa in the family room is the way to go. However, if you only host a large group once or twice a year, a more flexible furniture arrangement might work.

Last, decide on a color scheme, or base a room around a single element that is special to you.

Guidelines for Creating an Elegant but Comfortable Space

Keep it simple and take your time. Rooms thrown together in a day usually end up looking boring or over-accessorized and cluttered.

If you love something, you can find a place for it. But it's also okay if you have an empty space. Just keep looking. Don't settle for something because you think you have to fill a hole.

Don't be afraid to move things around from room to room. It's just redecorating for free. If it doesn't work out, you can always move it back.

Although it is important to have the things you love around your home, it's also smart to show restraint when placing items. A well-curated collection can be beautifully displayed on walls, shelves, or in cabinets. But a single vase or bowl on a bare table can be stunning as well.

To me, an elegant and livable space has everything you need and nothing you don't. But to be clear, I may need a lamp to read by, but I also need the antique desk it sits on because it belonged to my father and it is special to me. People have different needs, physical and mental. The ideal space mixes both in a way that makes beautiful things functional.

If there is something a client really wants, there is always a way to incorporate the idea. For example, if a client wants orange walls in her kitchen, that's energizing. If the client wants and needs that energy in her home, that's the starting point. Elegance can be achieved by keeping the other materials in the kitchen sleek and simple.

Let your home make you happy. Walking into your home should be like getting a hug. Or at least a welcoming pat on the back. I like spaces to be calm and happy places to come home to or to wake up in.

Style Elements that Create a Timeless and Classic Home Decor

Paying attention to the architectural finishes in a home is a large part of a timeless or classic look. They dictate what the interior can become.

Eclectic interiors can be beautiful, but forcing colonial-era furniture into an A-frame lodge in the mountains just doesn't sit well with me. It doesn't have to be one style over another, but find the right mix to represent someone's personality and lifestyle.

Classic interiors can have a good balance of traditional pieces that are updated with fresh fabrics and unique trimmings. For example, modern lacquered tables can feel less modern when paired with Windsor-backed dining chairs. Your grandmother's Chesterfield can be slipcovered in washable cotton until the kids get older. Then spring for that silk velvet upholstery.

Our homes are not museums – it's okay to mix up our exhibits a little bit.

SALLIE KJOS

*Make sure your furniture is made well, can withstand love
and lounging, and that it is comfortable.*

Identifying your Personal Style

Go through your favorite interior design magazines and pull out photographs that inspire you. Sometimes people are drawn to a variety of styles, but after assembling a collection of photographs, they might see a pattern emerge.

Consider your passions, hobbies, and interests. Those elements can be incorporated into artwork, accessories, and furniture style.

I pay attention to my clients' day-to-day grind. If they are on the go all the time, I want their home to have a peaceful feel so they have a place to unwind and relax, visually and physically.

Questions to Ask When Starting a Design Project

First I ask, "How are you going to use your space and who is going to use the space?" Families with children or pets need fabrics that clean easily and rugs that clean well or are soft for kids to sit on and play.

My second question is "Will you entertain?" That helps determine how much seating is needed and the right layout. If the answer is yes, I make the floor plans visually cohesive, so if you are entertaining in the family room, you can easily bring in chairs from the living room.

Third, what do you need from this space? Some people want bright color and energy, others want peace and tranquility, and some want both. That requires compromise, but it can easily be accomplished with accent color pops.

Guidelines for Creating an Elegant but Comfortable Space

Invest in great fabrics. Make sure your furniture is made well, can withstand love and lounging, and that it is comfortable. Down and fiber mixes are great for comfort and helping to hold shape. They look fabulous, but are also relaxing. Invest in fabric that feels good on the skin and is not rough, especially on your feet.

Choose an ottoman for your coffee table, with a tray on top for drinks and a throw underneath for a color pop, and put your feet up and relax.

Take your children's special artwork or pencil drawings and put them in antique frames and make a wall collage. It looks elegant in the frames and becomes priceless artwork that warms the heart.

Style Elements that Create a Timeless and Classic Home Decor

Your foundation choices, such as your flooring, tile, and paint colors are key. While unique flooring or tile choices can look wonderful and add a lot of interest, for a classic look, keep your design flair to accessories or an accent wall, using color, a stencil, or wallpaper.

Make sure that if you took everything out of your house, it would still look beautiful. Then you know you have a good foundation. It is a lot like make-up, actually: You need a great foundation as your base. Then you add the blush, which is your furniture. Keep them visually soft and neutral. Your lipstick is your color pop. That is your art, pillows, throws, accessories, vases, etc.

Your eyes are your lighting, what helps you see. Get rid of builder grade fixtures and invest in great lighting. This highlights and shows off all the pretty features and investments in your home.

SHARON KLEINMAN

It's important to choose pieces that are classic and timeless.
Stay away from anything too trendy.

Identifying your Personal Style

My goal is to create an interior that is unique to each client's needs and particular style. Defining how they wish to live in the space is the first step in helping the client to develop their own personal style. I have some clients who know exactly what they like, but for others it's a process.

Questions to Ask When Starting a Design Project

Before I begin a project, I ask lots of questions about how my clients like to utilize their living space.

- What are your hobbies?
- What activities do you do as a family?
- What do you do to unwind?
- Do you have particular heirlooms or cherished objects?
- Are there pieces of art that you wish to incorporate?

Guidelines for Creating an Elegant but Comfortable Space

Think about what colors you like to wear and how they make you feel. Also think about what emotions certain colors evoke. For example, soft blues, greens, and taupe make me feel serene.

Style Elements that Create a Timeless and Classic Home Decor

Whether you prefer traditional, transitional, or contemporary styles, it's important to choose pieces that are classic and timeless. Stay away from anything too trendy. Instead, choose furniture pieces with clean lines that can easily be incorporated into any type of design style. Color is totally personal.

Part of my role as an interior designer is to educate my clients, not only as to what's popular and available, but about proportion and scale, how to mix old with new, and what colors complement each other.

KAI TONG

Identifying your Personal Style

If I'm visiting clients in their home, I ask them to talk about what aspects of their surroundings they feel truly reflect their personal style and goals and why. I also ask them to point out what contradicts their perceived style and vision and why.

Some clients are more comfortable articulating their vision and style verbally. If they're not, we encourage them to gather photos and clippings, not only of styles that resonate with them, but also images they hate. This launches a dialogue about results that they absolutely do not want.

Questions to Ask When Starting a Design Project

Think about the intrinsic assets and liabilities of the space, such as views, connection to the rest of the house, utilities, etc. The time and budget parameters are also important.

Guidelines for Creating an Elegant but Comfortable Space

Create a master plan. It doesn't need to implemented and finished immediately, but it will allow the clients to live in the space and observe how both the space and their vision and needs evolve.

Style Elements that Create a Timeless and Classic Home Decor

The designer must understand and respect the existing architectural vocabulary of the client's home and spaces. Many clients want any improvements to be a continuation of that style. At the same time, other clients appreciate a design that is a graceful, dramatic, and/or seamless and an emancipating departure from the original aesthetic.

The designer must understand and respect the existing architectural
vocabulary of the client's home and spaces.

JESSICA PARKER WACHTEL

Identifying your Personal Style

A home should reflect those who live there. Don't get caught up in trying to recreate a space you've seen in a catalog or design magazine. Focus on your own taste and how you will really use the space.

Show off your interests and personality by displaying family photos, favorite books, artwork, or creating a grouping of items you collected while traveling.

There are no rules for what works. Just create a space that makes you happy.

Questions to Ask When Starting a Design Project

In addition to thinking about how you want a room to function, ask how you want this space to make you and your guests feel.

Don't get caught up in trying to recreate a space you've seen in a catalog or design magazine.

Guidelines for Creating an Elegant but Comfortable Space

Even the most elegant rooms should still be functional and inviting. Design your space with pieces you really love and don't be afraid to mix different styles.

Style Elements that Create a Timeless and Classic Home Decor

Bright walls may be fun for a few years, but to keep it refined and timeless, stick with a soft, neutral wall color and build from there.

Choose sturdy furniture with classic lines. Add texture and warmth with the right mix of lighting. And add a unique flare with something unexpected, such as a graphic rug that can be changed out over time.

*Don't be afraid
to mix
different styles.*

Add a unique flare with something unexpected...

MARIKA MEYER

Identifying your Personal Style

Weigh both form and function. Take an accurate account of how you use spaces on a daily basis and how you want them to look aesthetically. Decide if you're more traditional, contemporary, or in between, and how pieces will reflect your personal style.

Questions to Ask When Starting a Design Project

Once you determine how the space will be used, you can start selecting pieces to accommodate those needs. This is the functional side of design.

Guidelines for Creating an Elegant but Comfortable Space

This is where the aesthetics come in. It's important to do a little research. Determine what style you like, such as mid-century or contemporary. Also ask if that style is reflective of you? Think about how you can bring in art and accessories that are more reflective of your personal style, not something you've seen that might not be relevant to you.

Style Elements that Create a Timeless and Classic Home Decor

Design is an investment – you don't want to have to redesign spaces too often. Keep the lines of the pieces classic and tailored, with simple upholstery, and as elegant as possible to give the items longevity, sometimes ten to twenty years. This is especially true for sofas, club chairs, dining tables, side tables, chests, and coffee tables.

*Determine what style you like, such as
mid–century or contemporary.*

CHRISTIE LEU

Identifying your Personal Style

When rooms are inspired by things you love, they reflect your personal style, whether it is the shape of a piece of furniture, a color, a subject, or a piece of artwork.

Questions to Ask When Starting a Design Project

Look at your world: What attracts you? Find a way to insert that into your space. Then build around it, using the basic design principles.

*Everything you love does not need to be
included in every space. Edit.*

Guidelines for Creating an Elegant but Comfortable Space

Everything you love does not need to be included in every space. Edit. You want to have
variety in texture, shape, value, and size, but you do not need to show the depth of your
interests in one room. Your passions will have more impact if you spread them throughout
the house or several rooms. Group like things together. One room can have a travel focus,
another arts and music, animals, etc.

Style Elements that Create a Timeless and Classic Home Decor

If your furnishings are size-appropriate for the room, the space will almost always look good. Try to have only the things in a room that you will really use or look at and the design will be perfect for you.

ROBIN SPIRES

The best spaces reflect the homeowner's
interests and personality.

Identifying your Personal Style

Look at the way you dress: Is it easy and comfortable? Do you like things buttoned up and structured? Classic and neutral? Or do you prefer creativity? This is a first glimpse into your design style.

Questions to Ask When Starting a Design Project

Think about how you will use a room. Then the beauty and fun of design can begin.

Guidelines for Creating an Elegant but Comfortable Space

Involve yourself in the design process. Sit in the chairs and on the sofas. Feel the furnishings. Close your eyes and imagine living with the pieces.

Create a checklist of characteristics to use when comparing pieces of furniture.

Style Elements that Create a Timeless and Classic Home Decor

The best spaces reflect the homeowner's interests and personality. Collections and mementos are wonderful additions, but keep them edited and contained. The key is to allow pieces to be seen and not overwhelm or over decorate.

ABOUT THE CONTRIBUTORS

John Brown

John Brown has been involved in the design industry and with retail stores for over 30 years. He started his career in Springfield, Illinois, and for the past 15 years has based his design services out of his Old Town Alexandria shop: J. Brown & Co. He creates tailored, traditional and original environments for his clients. John is known for his choice of elegant Italian woven fabrics, quality furnishings, and bringing the outdoors in with the use of weathered garden statuary, flowers and plants. He has designed homes across the globe. He has also received numerous awards for design and civic achievements. John has two daughters and lives in Alexandria, Virginia. One of his daughters shares his love of design and has her own shop in Old Town.

Learn more about John's company on his Facebook page: www.facebook.com/pages/J-Brown-Co/246783155354669.

Molly Bruno

Molly Bruno, a native Washingtonian, has been a lifelong design enthusiast. Her aesthetic is traditional classic décor with vibrant and personal finishes. Pulling together tailored rooms with well-curated vignettes helps her create beautiful living spaces where great design really does live in the details.

Molly believes homes look their most beautiful when they reflect the personalities and lifestyles of the people who reside in them. Since opening her own firm in 2013, that's what she helps her clients achieve. Molly lives in the District with her husband Mike and their four children.

You can learn more about Molly on her website: www.mollybruno.com.

David Anthony Chenault

With 27 years in the interior design business, David Anthony has made his own collaboration of the Midwest Style and has fused it into projects around the country. His childhood was spent in Colorado and Missouri, which affords his work a warm and comfortable perspective, yet always keeping it luxe and current to compete with today's lifestyle. David Anthony is passionate about designing and it definitely shows throughout his work and in his personal life.

d² decorium design has been around for over 11 years, but David Anthony has been designing his entire life. When he was 10, he designed his first house out of a cardboard box — the drapery was made from paper towels and the furnishings from soda tops, building blocks, and other items found around the house. This memory reminds him that it is always important to remember our past, bring it forward, and by the infusing of the two, excitement will be brought to the project.

David Anthony was recently chosen by *Home & Design* magazine in their limited edition magazine *PORTFOLIO* as one of the Top 100 Designers in the tri-state area [100 = 35 architects, 35 designers, and 30 landscape designers].

You can connect with David Anthony through his website: www.d2-interiordesign.com.

Missy Deerin

Since 2005, Missy has worked with families and individuals to create beautiful and functional interior design for both home and office spaces. Missy strives to design interiors that are well-organized and uncluttered, minding the client's personal style in every detail.

Born and raised in the Washington, D.C., area, Missy lives in Chevy Chase, Maryland, with her husband and three children.

You can learn more about Missy's services on her website: www.missydeerindesigns.com.

Kerra Michele Huerta

Kerra Michele is an interior designer, event designer, and self-described "long-time renter" in Washington, D.C., and has developed a knack for space planning, organization, and clever design ideas that anyone can implement. Her life is dedicated to improving lifestyles (especially of those who are renting the American Dream) and creating unique, special spaces — whether that space be in your home or at an event.

You can follow her blog, *Apartment Envy*, at www.aptenvy.com.

Kerrie Kelly

Northern California interior designer Kerrie Kelly founded Kerrie Kelly Design Lab in 1995. She is an award-winning interior designer, author and multi-media consultant, helping national brands reach the interior design market. She is a certified interior designer with an Interior Design degree from Cal Poly, San Luis Obispo and has a Master's in Business Administration.

A member of ASID (American Society of Interior Designers), NKBA (National Kitchen and Bath Association) and IIDA (International Interior Design Association), Kerrie is a Certified Aging in Place Specialist (CAPS), sits on the Advisory Board for Eskaton's Livable Design and is an avid representative and speaker for Livable Design's initiatives. She has authored two books: *Home Decor: A Sunset Design Guide* and *My Interior Design Kit* with Pearson Professional and Career Education.

Kerrie is one of four national Subject Matter Experts (SME) for Home Depot. She serves as a member of the Design Advisory Board at *Zillow, Inc.* and contributes monthly articles for their website, reaching *Yahoo!*, *Forbes*, and *Wall Street Journal*. She also writes a monthly column for *Sparefoot* and *Style Media Group*.

She was named the 2012 recipient of ASID's Nancy Vincent McClelland Merit Award for Interior Design Education and has received several local ASID residential design awards. She also received Houzz's Best of Remodeling Award in 2012 and Best of Design and Customer Satisfaction Awards in 2013 and 2014.

Check out her website at www.kerriekelly.com.

Sallie Kjos

Sallie Kjos is a northern Virginia based accomplished interior designer who has worked in the design field for over 20 years. From a very early age, she learned to appreciate the true quality and craftsmanship of antiques, working in her aunt's quaint home specialty boutique, The English Cottage. It was during this time that she discovered her passion for combining antiques with the simple treasures of today. These ideas would soon transpire into a unique interior design business, creating design plans for clients to envision and experience in their own homes.

In 2009, Sallie started GreyHunt Interiors, which offers elegant and exclusive designs, connecting the dots to create a flow of style in homes. Each design project reflects the understanding of the client's ideas, as well as creating "the look" for that fresh and inviting home. The most important part for Sallie is to really hear her clients and reflect them so they truly feel at home in their space. Sallie knows that what makes a home is the family. That is why she named her business "Grey" for Greyson and "Hunt" for Hunter, her two sons, because the heart is where the home is. Sallie believes that function and design are key in making a cohesive space.

Learn more about Sallie and her services through her website: www.greyhuntinteriors.com.

Sharon Kleinman

Designer Sharon Kleinman brings her clients' dreams to reality through the home design business she founded more than fifteen years ago. Over the past several years, Sharon's interior design work for her clients, as well as her own home, have been featured in *Washington Home & Design Magazine*, "Spectacular Homes of Greater Washington, D.C.," and *Home & Design*, "Portfolio of Top Designers."

In projects ranging from kitchen redesigns to whole house makeovers to full designs for homes under construction, Sharon brings excitement, passion, expertise and an exacting attention to detail to the design process. Above all, her desire is for her clients to put their own personal stamp on their homes. "Each interior should reflect the client's style, not mine," she says.

Sharon believes that thorough planning is the key to a well-designed room, and that the best rooms evolve over time. She begins the design process by asking her clients to list what they want to do in a given room: watch television, read a book, listen to music, or play games, for example. Then she develops options to incorporate her clients' wish list. Once they agree on a plan, she begins selecting furniture, window treatments and wall finishes in line with her clients' tastes.

Sharon often frequents antique shops, retail stores and art galleries, looking for just the right items which will reflect the clients' aesthetics and puts the finishing touches on every interior she helps create.

Learn more about Sharon on her website: www.4transitions.com.

Anna Kucera

Anna Kucera is the owner of and principal designer for Gracious Living by Design. Her knowledge and experience translates to a reassuring design process for her clients. Anna has a Master of Fine Arts degree in Interior Design and has worked extensively with luxury lifestyle companies. This combination of skills allows her to provide clients with a sophisticated design and a personalized experience. She was a Best of Houzz 2014 Winner and was voted 2013 Best Interior Designer in Northern Virginia by *Virginia Living* readers.

You can learn more about Anna on her website: www.graciouslivingbydesign.com.

Christie Leu

Christie Leu of Christie Leu Interiors began her career as an artist and spent time working in fine functional craft. After getting married and having five children, she made a career change, receiving a degree in interior design with a focus on kitchens and baths. As a student, she was honored for her work by the National Kitchen and Bath Association.

Christie lives in Chevy Chase, Maryland, with her husband and five children, which includes a set of triplets.

Allie Mann

Allie Mann is a D.C. native doing what she loves: designing beautiful bathrooms and kitchens. When she's not designing for Case, she's teaching Kitchen and Bathroom Design at Northern Virginia Community College in Sterling, VA. And when she's not doing that, she's beaching it with her husband Matt and their puppy Colby at Rehoboth Beach in DE. And when she's not doing that, she's pursuing what she really loves: baking and designing sweets. Watch out Georgetown Cupcake!

Allie began her professional career in 2004 as a visual merchandise manager for a high-end furniture retailer. She joined Case Design Remodeling in 2005 as a designer. She's currently a kitchen and bath designer with Case and has held this role since 2010.

Allie Mann earned her Bachelor of Fine Arts in Interior Design/Studio Art from James Madison University. Allie joined Case Design/Remodeling, Inc. in 2005 and began specializing in kitchen and bath design in 2010. She is an Allied Member of the American Society of Interior Designers, a NARI Certified Kitchen and Bathroom Remodeler, Green Advantage Certified, and a member of the Adjunct Faculty at Northern Virginia Community College where she teaches IDS 293 Kitchen and Bath Studies as part of the Interior Design Program.

Allie won a Rising Star Award at Case, a NARI CotY Award for one of her DC Design House spaces, and has been featured in numerous publications including *The Washington Post, Kitchen & Bath Ideas, Home & Design, Designline, Metro Washington Home Improvement,* and *Elan.* She was also a featured builder/designer for *Extreme Makeover: Home Edition* in 2010. For the past four years, Allie has been selected to participate in the DC Design House, DC's premiere show house benefiting Children's National Health System, as well as in two recent Georgetown Jingles, which benefits Georgetown University Hospital Center Pediatrics.

Connect with Allie through this website: www.casedesign.com/bio/allie-mann

Melissa Mather

Melissa Mather has spent the last ten years writing about interior design for magazines in San Francisco and London.

Marika Meyer

Practical luxury, functional beauty: Marika Meyer Interiors is a full-service interior design firm specializing in residential design. With each client's lifestyle and taste in mind, Marika references the architectural integrity of each project to encourage harmony between structure and decoration, artfully mixing classic and transitional elements. The result: beautifully proportioned environments that are elegant and sophisticated yet welcoming, livable, and absolutely personal...the very definition of feeling right at home.

A native Washingtonian, Marika established the firm in 2007, a culmination of her formal interior design education and practical experience in the interior design industry. She was named "One to Watch" by the Washington Design Center in 2012, called a "Hot Talent" by *Home & Design* magazine in 2011, and has been on Martha Stewart Living Radio. Marika has also been featured in numerous publications including *The Washington Post, Traditional Home, House Beautiful, HGTV, Luxe, Interiors, American Lifestyle, Bethesda, Washingtonian, Washingtonian MOM,* and *Northern Virginia* magazines. Marika was also selected to participate in the 2012 and 2014 DC Design Houses, DC's premiere show house benefitting Children's National Health System.

Learn more about Marika and her services on her website: www.meyerinteriors.com.

Ann O'Shields

Ann O'Shields is the owner of The Nest Egg in Fairfax, VA, a home furnishings boutique and interior design business. Since 2004, Ann has been working with customers and clients in the VA/DC/MD area to provide a unique shopping experience and to create their ideal interior spaces. The Nest Egg offers custom upholstery and case goods with a focus on domestic made items. Artwork, rugs, lighting, home accessories and gift items are plentiful with new merchandise arriving weekly in the retail store.

The Nest Egg's interior design services offer full room designs including furniture and accessories as well as flooring, paint, window treatments, light fixtures and all of the details to make a space complete. Ann and her staff focus on creating livable spaces that are comfortable, current, and have personality to reflect those who live there.

Ann's role includes all merchandise buying for the store, manufacturer relationships, marketing and advertising, as well as managing the interior design business. Prior to opening The Nest Egg, Ann spent 10+ years in advertising, marketing and business strategy, working as part of an in-house marketing team for a retail store, inside an advertising agency, and in interactive marketing, working with clients in the publishing and travel categories.

Learn more at http://shopthenestegg.blogspot.com/.

Victoria Sanchez

Victoria began her career nearly 30 years ago, specializing in residential design in the Washington, D.C., area. Her experience has led to major projects all over the region and expanded into commercial design, space planning and home staging for realtors. Her design services include pre-construction strategy and materials specification along with interior decoration.

Victoria has both an undergraduate and masters degree in interior design from Marymount University in Arlington, VA. She also teaches interior design courses at local colleges.

Learn more about Victoria's services on her website: www.victoriaathome.com.

Robin Spires

Robin Spires is the owner of The Robin's Nest, where her goal is to create interior spaces that please the eye and the soul. She is passionate about preserving the quality and personality of what is often discarded and seen as unusable. In business since 2006, The Robin's Nest relocated to Maryland in 2010.

Robin has a strong desire to share as many artisan-made products as possible. She carries updated vintage elements and hand-selected items to allow customers to achieve a one-of-a-kind look. Pillows, home accessories and vintage items are specially chosen with her customers in mind.

You can learn more about Robin and The Robin's Nest at www.therobinsnesthome.com.

Courtney Thomas

Courtney Thomas is the owner of The Picket Fence, a family-run boutique located in Burke, VA. The Picket Fence offers a unique variety of home accessories and gifts for every occasion.

Check out her blog at www.shopthepicketfence.blogspot.com.

Kai Tong

With 25 years of experience as both an architect and builder for demanding high-end custom residential clientele in Washington's finest neighborhoods, Kai makes your dreams take form with empathy, creativity, and a profound respect for the client and the process.

Kai's first project was one of the very first modern façade commercial designs to be approved in historic Georgetown. And it went on to win a national design award from *Interior Design Magazine*.

After a couple of extremely successful decades working on his own, Kai joined Maryland-based firm Hopkins & Porter Construction in 2000, and now serves as Director of Architectural Services for their Architecture Department.

Learn more about Kai's services through Hopkins & Porter's website: www.hopkinsandporter.com.

Jessica Parker Wachtel

A native of the Washington, D.C. area, Jessica Parker Wachtel has been passionate about interior design her whole life. After graduating with a degree in Interior Design from Indiana University, she has been professionally designing interiors, both commercial and residential, for nearly 10 years. She is a LEED Accredited Professional and strives to design in an environmentally friendly manner. Jessica also was selected to participate in the 2013 DC Design House, DC's premiere show house benefitting Children's National Health System.

Jessica joined the team at GTM Architects in 2006, and has since worked on many prestigious homes throughout the Washington, D.C. area. GTM Architects, located in Bethesda, MD, is a full service, award-winning architecture and design firm serving clients in the D.C. region and nationwide. Established in 1989, GTM's primary objective has always been a commitment to excellence in both service and design. Jessica, a Project Designer II, and the GTM team produce thoughtful and creative design solutions that respond to the needs of each individual client.

You can connect with Jessica through GTM's website: www.gtmarchitects.com.

PHOTOGRAPHY CREDITS

Victoria Sanchez
Photography by Robert Radifera

Ann O'Shields
Photography by Ann O'Shields

David Anthony Chenault
Photography by David Anthony Chenault

John Brown
Photography by John Brown and Sandra Caughlin

Kerrie Kelley
Photography by Brian Kellogg Photography

Kerra Michele Huerta
Photography by Kerra Michele Huerta

Courtney Thomas
Photography by Courtney Thomas

Molly Bruno
Photography by Brian Searby

Allie Mann
Photography by June Stanich and Alain Jaramillo for Case Design/Remodeling, Inc.

Missy Deerin
Photography by Missy Deerin

Sallie Kjos
Photography by Sallie Kjos, GreyHunt Interiors

Sharon Kleinman
Photography by Gwin Hunt

Kai Tong
Photography by John Troha Photography

Jessica Parker Wachtel
Photography by Ken Wyner and Diego Valdez

Marika Meyer
Photography by Angie Seckinger

Christine Leu
Project Designed by Hamilton Snowber Architects
Photography by Stacy Zarin Goldberg

Robin Spires
Photography by Robin Spires, The Robin's Nest

CPSIA information can be obtained at www.ICGtesting.com
Printed in the USA
BVOW11*2216131114

375069BV00006B/8/P